SO-ABA-682

THE TRANSCONTINENTAL
RAILROAD

Essential Events

THE TRANSCONTINENTAL RAILROAD

BY DIANE GIMPEL

Content Consultant
Eric Morser, assistant professor of history
Skidmore College

ABDO
Publishing Company

CREDITS

Published by ABDO Publishing Company, 8000 West 78th Street,
Edina, Minnesota 55439. Copyright © 2011 by Abdo Consulting
Group, Inc. International copyrights reserved in all countries. No
part of this book may be reproduced in any form without written
permission from the publisher. The Essential Library™ is a
trademark and logo of ABDO Publishing Company.

Printed in the United States of America,
North Mankato, Minnesota
112010
012011

 THIS BOOK CONTAINS AT LEAST 10% RECYCLED MATERIALS.

Editor: Amy Van Zee
Copy Editor: Paula Lewis
Interior Design and Production: Kazuko Collins
Cover Design: Kazuko Collins

Library of Congress Cataloging-in-Publication Data
Gimpel, Diane, 1963-
 The transcontinental railroad / by Diane Gimpel.
    p. cm. -- (Essential events)
 Includes bibliographical references and index.
 ISBN 978-1-61714-768-5
 1. Pacific railroads--History--Juvenile literature. 2. Railroads
--United States--History--Juvenile literature. 3. Railroads--
West (U.S.)--History--Juvenile literature. I. Title.
 TF25.P23G56 2011
 385.0973--dc22
                        2010044830

TABLE OF CONTENTS

Pioneer photographer Andrew Russell captured the historic moment
when Union Pacific joined with Central Pacific in 1869.

MISSION ACCOMPLISHED

During the afternoon of Monday, May 10, 1869, telegraph operators throughout the United States waited for word of a momentous change from a remote spot in northern Utah. That spot was Promontory Summit. From there, telegraph

operator Watson N. Shilling sent a
message nationwide: "Almost ready.
Hats off. Prayer is being offered."[1]
A telegraph operator in Chicago,
Illinois, responded: "We understand.
All are ready in the east."[2]

Another message was sent from
Promontory: "All ready now. The
spike will soon be driven. The
signal will be three dots for the
commencement of the blow."[3]
Then, at 12:47 p.m. in Utah,
Shilling tapped out three dots.
It meant: Done.

Old Gives Way to New

The day before the two parts of the transcontinental railroad were joined, a newspaper reporter noted a horse-pulled stagecoach delivering mail at Promontory Summit, a job that would henceforth be done by train. "With that dusty, dilapidated coach and team, the old order of things passed away forever," the reporter wrote.[4]

Spread internationally, that word meant
the last spike had been driven in approximately
2,000 miles (3,200 km) of a new railroad that
connected existing railroads in the eastern part of
the United States to California in the West. This
connection shortened travel between the East and
West coasts to an affordable, weeklong journey that
had once been expensive and taken several months.
The railroad opened the vast wilderness in the
middle of the continent not only to settlement by
millions of European Americans but also to millions

of dollars in trade. Named the Pacific Railroad, it was North America's first transcontinental railroad, and it would have an indelible impact on the development of the United States.

CONNECTION MADE

The Central Pacific Railroad Company and the Union Pacific Railroad Company were formed expressly for this project. Central Pacific, led by the company's president and California Governor Leland Stanford, built eastward from

The Telegraph

Intertwined with the history of the railroad is the development of the telegraph, which can send messages instantly using electricity. Like the steam-driven locomotive railroads, electric telegraphy developed in the early nineteenth century. Many believed the communication method could help unite the nation.

Once the railway age began in the 1830s, railroad operators needed a way to send instant messages to manage the traffic of trains traveling in both directions on single tracks. A telegraph system invented by William Fothergill Cooke and Charles Wheatstone was used for that purpose for the first time in England in 1837. In the United States, Samuel Morse developed a telegraph device in which the electric current flowing through a wire was interrupted for short periods—called dots—or long periods—called dashes—by holding down a key. The dots and dashes were configured into codes that could be translated by the receiver.

The first US telegraph lines were strung along the Baltimore & Ohio Railroad. Telegraph wires reached from coast to coast by 1861 and played an important part in the American Civil War. Couriers were no longer necessary to transmit important messages. Instead, generals and leaders could rely on a much faster method of communication.

Sacramento, California, beginning in 1863. Union Pacific, led in large part by the company's vice president Thomas Durant, built westward from Omaha, Nebraska, beginning the same year. When it came time to join the two portions, executives from each company traveled by train to the connection site in Utah. Central Pacific executives had already arrived at Promontory Summit by the time the Union Pacific train arrived on the morning of May 10, 1869. Also on hand for the event were newspaper reporters, photographers, railroad workers from a variety of ethnicities, soldiers, bands, and other spectators.

Pullman Makes Train Travel Luxurious

Author David Haward Bain described the car carrying Thomas Durant and the Union Pacific faction as a "sumptuous Pullman palace car."[5] The railcar was named for its developer, George Pullman, who created elegant sleeping cars with pillows and sheets and dining cars. A Pullman car was used to return President Abraham Lincoln's body to Illinois after his assassination.

The ceremony to mark the linking of the two lines began with Central Pacific workers laying a railroad tie. This piece of wood is used to secure the metal rails upon which the wheels of railroad cars and engines roll. A ceremonial tie made in California of laurel wood, unlike the pine typically used, was placed by the two men who supervised construction for the two railroad companies.

Two final rails were put in place—one by a Union Pacific gang and the other by a Central Pacific gang.

The rails were to be secured to the last tie with four ceremonial spikes. Of the two gold spikes, one was inscribed with the words "The Last Spike" and "May God continue the unity of our country as this railroad unites the two great Oceans of the world."[6] The job of installing the gold spikes went to Stanford, who used a special, silver-topped hammer to do the job. Durant installed two ceremonial spikes. One was silver, and the other was iron covered in gold and silver. The four precious metal spikes and laurel tie then were removed and replaced with a pine tie and four iron spikes for the telegraph procedure. One of these was wired to the transcontinental telegraph line, as was the iron hammer that drove it in. The plan was that when the spike and the hammer met, the telegraph circuit would be completed and the message of the railroad's completion would go out. As it turned out, it was Shilling, the telegraph operator, who tapped the three dots to signal "done."

Spikes on Display

Following the joining of the rails, the four ceremonial spikes were removed. The main golden spike and a silver spike now reside in Palo Alto, California, at Stanford University, which was founded by Central Pacific president Leland Stanford. An iron spike with gold on its head and silver on its shaft is now owned by the Museum of the City of New York. The location of the second gold spike used in the ceremony is unknown.

In the mid-nineteenth century, settlers moving West traveled by horse-drawn wagons. The transcontinental railroad expedited travel West.

A soldier in the area named J. W. Malloy expressed awe by saying, "We stood with mouths agape as we realized that the much talked-of line was completed."[7]

CELEBRATION

The telegraph message intentionally set off alarm bells in cities across the country. Cannons fired in San Francisco and New York City. Church bells pealed, fire bells rang, and train whistles shrieked and screeched in cities such as Philadelphia, Pennsylvania, and Buffalo, New York. During the

Promontory celebration, Central Pacific official James Campbell gave the last speech in which he stated, "Little you realize what you have done. You have this day changed the path of commerce and finance of the whole world."[8]

What Really Happened?

Although photographers and newspaper reporters were present at the Promontory Summit joining ceremony, accounts about what happened that day differ. For example, some, including the Golden Spike National Historic Site, say Central Pacific's Leland Stanford and Union Pacific's Thomas Durant missed when they struck at the ceremonial last spikes. Historian David Haward Bain, however, contends no evidence of that occurrence exists.

The celebrations at Promontory Summit and throughout the United States hailed a mode of transportation that changed how people and goods traveled across the country and, as a result, changed the country itself. Construction of the transcontinental railroad had begun during a tumultuous political situation: the American Civil War. The North and South had been fiercely polarized during the four-year conflict. But the transcontinental railroad, completed four years after the end of the war, would help rebuild the wounded nation. The railroad culminated six years of construction and made real the dreams that had been dreamt long before work had begun.

Thomas Durant and other Union Pacific executives traveled to Promontory Summit in a Pullman car.

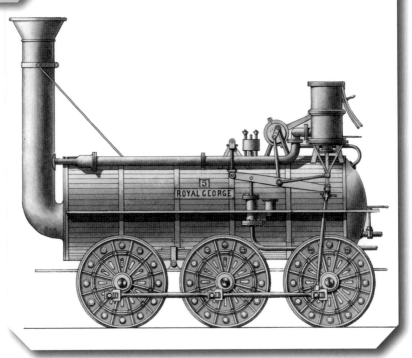

An early steam locomotive, circa 1827

THE RISE OF THE TRAIN

The building of the transcontinental railroad was part of a broader transportation revolution that was taking place in nineteenth-century North America. When Europeans settled on the continent in the late fifteenth century, they relied upon animals, wind- or man-powered ships, and walking to take them from place to place. By the nineteenth century, modes and methods of transportation began to change as US pioneers pushed westward.

In 1825, the Erie Canal was opened, ushering in social and economic change. This waterway connected the Great Lakes to the Atlantic Ocean. It improved ease of trade and aided in the development of cities along the waterway. Boats sailing on the canal traveled much more quickly than wagons, which were pulled by horses that could carry a limited amount of goods.

The Erie Canal connected people in the Great Lakes region to people on the East Coast. In the early nineteenth century, larger groups of settlers began moving from the New England states into the Great Lakes regions and closer to the Mississippi River. And by the middle of the century, pioneers had begun to settle the California coast.

Traveling to the West Coast was difficult, however. People crossing

George Washington and Julius Caesar

Prior to the transportation innovations of the late eighteenth and early nineteenth centuries, the means for travel had not changed much in thousands of years. "George Washington had no better means of travel than had Julius Caesar, or the Pharaohs of ancient Egypt," wrote railroad historian John Debo Galloway.[1]

Conestoga Wagons

The covered wagons pioneers used to travel West were called Conestoga wagons, named for the Pennsylvania town from which they originated. Conestoga wagons were recognizable by their bowed cover. This shape made it less likely for contents to shift as the wagons traveled over hills. The large wheels prevented contents from becoming wet when the wagons crossed a stream.

the country used covered wagons. But even with wagons, people mostly walked. The wagons, pulled slowly by oxen, carried household goods, food, the young, and the infirm. The difficult journey took months. Travelers faced dangers such as running out of water and food, experiencing bad weather, and running afoul of American Indians who did not want settlers invading their lands.

Another way to reach California from the East Coast was to travel south by boat on the Atlantic Ocean to Panama in Central America. The traveler could then make an overland crossing at the Isthmus of Panama—a strip of land that connects North America and South America—and resume boat travel north on the Pacific Ocean to California. A third option was to make the journey entirely by water, traveling by boat around the tip of South America and then north to California. However, traveling through the Isthmus of Panama or the boat journey around South America were expensive, dangerous, and time-consuming options.

STEAM ENGINES AND LOCOMOTIVES

As people moved around on new routes and to new places on the North American continent, innovations in transportation became necessary. The first of the pivotal inventions was the steam-powered engine. Developed in the first part of the eighteenth century and refined in the 1770s by Scotsman James Watt, it helped bring up ore and water from England's coal and tin mines. Once steam power was harnessed successfully, people

Panama's Railroad and Canal

The world's first transcontinental railroad was built in Panama, the southernmost country in North America. Americans built it, in part, to accommodate those who wanted to go to California following the discovery of gold in 1849. Work on the railroad began in 1850. Twenty months later, only seven miles (11.3 km) of track had been laid. Construction was greatly hampered by the effects of mosquito-borne illnesses, which were a danger to anyone who came into the area. During the construction of the railroad, thousands of workers died from these illnesses. In addition, it was difficult to build on Panama's terrain, and the railroad company was broke. Nonetheless, prospectors paid to use the seven miles (11.3 km) of finished railroad, giving the enterprise a way to make money and finish the job. Work finished on the 47-mile- (76-km-) long line in 1855.

While the railroad could accommodate passengers and cargo, interest still existed in creating a canal through Panama to allow ships to pass between the Atlantic and Pacific Oceans. The French tried to build a canal in Panama at the end of the nineteenth century but abandoned the project. In 1904, the Americans undertook the job, finishing it in ten years. Now owned by the country of Panama, the canal continues to operate today. More than 13,000 ships use it annually.

American Peter Cooper built the Tom Thumb locomotive that raced against a horse in August 1830.

wondered whether it could power boats, which had relied upon wind power. In the United States, John Fitch first used a steam engine to propel a boat on the Delaware River north of Philadelphia in 1787. The invention did not gain popularity until after Robert Fulton built a steamboat that traveled the Hudson River in New York in the early nineteenth century. This got some people thinking. If a steam engine could propel vehicles in the water, why not on land?

The first railroads, constructed in the early nineteenth century, relied upon animal power rather than steam power. Horses pulled carts full of ore or coal on rails. England was the first to use steam-powered locomotives on land-based railways in the first decades of the nineteenth century following George Stephenson's 1814 invention of the first steam engine that was powered to ride on a railroad. Stephenson later developed the first public railway, the Stockton & Darlington, in 1825.

America's train history begins around 1830 when a steam locomotive named Tom Thumb, invented by Peter Cooper of New York, raced a horse—and lost. Yet, despite the loss, American-made locomotives soon replaced horses at the heads of trains. The Tom Thumb rode on the Baltimore & Ohio Railroad, the first commercial railroad in the United States. Also in 1830, a steam-driven train in South Carolina named the Best Friend of Charleston became the first train to carry passengers.

TROUBLES WITH TRAINS

Trains became popular because they were swifter than the alternatives, but they were not

Steamboats

Before steam engines revolutionized land travel, they revolution-ized water travel, which previously had relied on human muscle and the wind. After Robert Fulton established his steamboat line in New York in the early nineteenth century, steamboats soon made ocean voyages. By the mid-nineteenth century, steamboats made regular transatlantic trips.

without downsides. Early train travel was unreliable and did not always follow schedules. Additionally, train travel was noisy and uncomfortable. Trains had bench seats, little light provided by candles, little heat provided by wood- or coal-burning stoves, and poor ventilation due to shuttered windows. English author Charles Dickens described a ride he took on a Massachusetts train in the early 1840s: "There is a great deal of jolting, a great deal of noise, a great deal of wall, not much window, a locomotive engine, a shriek, and a bell."[2] Dickens further described the train cars as "shabby omnibuses" that could hold up to 50 people and had at their centers a red-hot stove.[3] By his description in his 1842 *American Notes*, Dickens apparently was sitting quite near to it: "It is insufferably close; and you see the hot air fluttering between yourself and any other object you may happen to look at, like the ghost of smoke."[4]

Train travel was also dangerous. Sparks from the train's smokestack could cause fires and were known to set ablaze passengers' clothing. The candles used for light and the stoves used for heat caused fires too. Due to the jerky motion of the trains, railroad workers suffered gruesome and sometimes fatal injuries. Railroads were also accident prone. Among the tragic accidents was an 1853 train wreck in Massachusetts. The 11-year-old son of President Franklin Pierce was killed just before Pierce's inauguration. And the problems with trains extended beyond the rails. Locomotives made so much smoke that the downwind side of tracks through a town often became the poorer side, leading to the saying "the wrong side of the tracks."

INVENTIONS BRING IMPROVEMENT

But improvements to train travel would soon come. Inventions made in the first decades of train travel in the United States included equalizing beams, which helped keep trains on rough tracks, and the switchback, which allowed locomotives to climb steep inclines. Rail bridges came into use beginning in 1840, although they were unsafe in the early decades and often the cause of tragic accidents.

Lincoln and Railroad Bridges

In 1856, Rock Island Bridge Company built the first rail bridge across the Mississippi River, an innovation necessary for a transcontinental railroad. When a steamboat ran into one of the piers and burned, the steamboat owner sued the bridge company. While the city of St. Louis, Missouri, and other river interests supported free navigation for boats, Chicago and the railroad interests supported the right of a railway to have a bridge.

Abraham Lincoln, a lawyer who had not yet sought election to the US presidency, represented the bridge company in an 1857 trial that left the jury deadlocked, leading the court to dismiss the case. The dismissal was considered a railroad victory. An Iowa court later ordered the bridge removed, but the Supreme Court overruled the Iowa court, declaring railroads could bridge rivers.

As the new mode of transportation experienced trials, tribulations, and triumphs, railroads became popular. By 1835, almost 1,000 miles (1,600 km) of track had been laid in the United States. By 1840, the United States had nearly 3,000 miles (4,800 km) of track, more than in all of Europe. By 1850, that figure was more than 9,000 miles (14,500 km), and by 1860, more than 30,000 miles (48,300 km) of track had been built in the United States. All of it was east of the Mississippi and Missouri Rivers. ⌐

British inventor and engineer George Stephenson, born in 1781,
finished his first locomotive in 1814.

An illustration shows the chaos created by a train traveling through Philadelphia, Pennsylvania, in the 1850s.

IDEA HATCHED;
ROUTE CHOSEN

*I*n February 1832, not quite two years after the Tom Thumb locomotive lost its race to a horse on the new Baltimore & Ohio Railroad, an editorial in the *Emigrant* in Ann Arbor, Michigan, stated:

It is in our power to build up an immense city at the mouth of the Oregon, to make it the depot for our East India trade & perhaps for that of Europe—in fact to unite New York and the Oregon by a rail way by which the traveler leaving the City of New York shall at the moderate rate of ten miles an hour, place himself in a port right on the shores of the Pacific. [1]

And so it was that almost immediately after steam-powered locomotives began riding the rails in the United States, the call went up for a railroad to span the continent. When the editorial was published, only two railroads were in operation in the United States with fewer than 200 miles (320 km) of track between them.

Railroad Advocates

Because of that editorial, the *Emigrant*'s editor, Samuel Dexter, was named the first proponent of the idea of a transcontinental railroad by *National Parks* magazine. Others supported the idea, including Hartwell Carver of New York and Samuel Bancroft Barlow of Massachusetts, both of whom were physicians. They wrote to newspapers to announce their support. Carver's idea was that the railroad would "be the means of uniting the whole world in one great church, a part of whose worship will be to praise God and bless the Oregon Railroad."[2] These religious reasons for building the railroad were later referred to as "manifest destiny."

One of the best-known proponents was New York merchant Asa Whitney. He not only advocated construction of a transcontinental railroad, but in 1844, he also asked the US Congress to let him build it. In 1849, Whitney published his proposal, *A Project for a Railroad to the Pacific*, to win over the public's support. His plan was to build the railroad line from Lake Michigan to the West Coast in exchange for land along the

Manifest Destiny

In the 1830s, Samuel Bancroft Barlow of Massachusetts asserted religious reasons for building a transcontinental railroad, and he was not alone in that way of thinking. Many of European descent in the eastern part of the United States believed God gave them the right and duty to settle and dominate the North American continent. The philosophy was called "manifest destiny" following the labeling of it as such by journalist John L. O'Sullivan in 1845. In a *United States Magazine and Democratic Review* editorial commenting upon the United States' annexation of Texas, O'Sullivan wrote about America's "manifest destiny to overspread the continent allotted by Providence for the free development of our multiplying millions."[3]

Manifest destiny assumed not only that those Americans of European ancestry had the God-given duty to settle the West but also that it was their duty to establish their democratic and Protestant religious values there to the exclusion of others, particularly those of Mexican descent and the American-Indian people.

route that he could sell to finance the project. Whitney characterized the railroad as a means to help trade between Asia and Europe, just as the early editorial in the *Emigrant* had done. Whitney also characterized a transcontinental railroad as a way to settle the continent. "This great work, this great and important change for the benefit of the entire human family," Whitney wrote, would:

> Open to settlement and production a wilderness of more than 2,000 miles, give to it cheap and rapid transit to, and communication with, all the markets of the world, all within our own command and control.[4]

Whitney did not convince the federal government to go along with his plan. Nonetheless, he generated support for the idea among both the public and its politicians. For example, Senator Stephen Douglas became a proponent of building the railroad.

Finding a Route

Once the US Congress became interested in the idea of a

California Gold Rush

One reason US citizens wanted a railroad to California was because the area had become settled following the discovery of gold. On January 24, 1848, men building a sawmill along the American River near Sacramento found tiny gold nuggets. That discovery was followed by other gold strikes in the next few years, bringing 500,000 immigrants to California, looking for riches.

transcontinental railroad, the next challenge was to decide where it should be built. Some congressmen who favored the idea wanted it to go through their districts where it would benefit them the most. To resolve the matter, in 1853, Congress gave US Secretary of War Jefferson Davis the job of establishing a route for the railroad and authorized $150,000 for exploration and surveying. Three years later, and after $340,000 had been spent, Davis submitted a report that included five possible routes, three of which were in the Northern part of the country and two of which were in the South.

Jefferson Davis

Jefferson Davis, who was in charge of finding possible routes for the transcontinental railroad in the 1850s, later became president of the Confederate States of America. This was the government formed by the Southern states that seceded from the Union in 1861. When the Confederacy lost the Civil War, Davis was imprisoned for two years and then released on bail. Criminal charges against him were dropped.

Both the Democratic and the Republican political parties called the construction of a transcontinental railroad a priority in the 1856 and 1860 presidential races. But, as was the case with many issues of the day, Congress was divided in Northern and Southern factions—particularly on issues such as slavery and states' rights. A Northern route would help the Northern industrial economy, placing the South at an economic disadvantage. A Southern route would expand the Southern economy, which was based upon plantation farming and required slave labor. Such a route could expand the practice of slavery, which many in the North opposed.

"Crazy Judah"

As the idea of a transcontinental railroad took hold in the US government, engineer Theodore Judah worked on early railroad projects. He first worked in the northeastern United States, which was the part of the country where he grew up. Then, in 1854, he was asked to go to California to help build the Sacramento Valley Railroad, the first railroad in the West. As he worked on other railroad projects in California, he began talking about building a cross-country railroad to the Pacific Ocean. He expressed so much enthusiasm for the project that some called him "Crazy Judah." He traveled several times to Washington DC to lobby Congress for the project. But Congress, which remained divided on issues such as the route the railroad would take, took no action on the idea as the nation moved closer to civil war.

Judah moved forward nonetheless. He sought and received California's support for the project.

Donner Pass

Donner Pass is a path through the Sierra Nevada mountain chain near Lake Tahoe in California. It is named for a pioneering group comprised of 89 members of the Donner family. Traveling from Illinois to California in 1846, a blizzard stranded them in the snow from October through December. Half of the people died. After eating their animals, some of the remaining members resorted to cannibalism to survive.

He sought investors. He also sought a passage for the railroad through the Sierra Nevada Mountains, a major obstacle for a rail line. In the fall of 1860, with the help of his assistant Daniel Strong, Judah examined the Donner Pass, which was located in the Sierra Nevada. There, a railroad would have only one mountain to ascend and descend. Everywhere else along the range, the railroad would have to ascend and descend two mountains to cross the range. Judah realized that Donner Pass was the most practical place to build a railroad route through the central part of the country.

In November 1860, Republican Abraham Lincoln was elected president of the United States, an event that was followed by the secession of the Southern states in 1861. As the Southern lawmakers were no longer a part of Congress, the idea that the railroad would be built through the South was no longer an option. But there were still obstacles to overcome before building could begin.

Theodore Judah worked in railroad jobs until he died in 1863.

In addition to serving as president of Central Pacific, Leland Stanford was a politician. He became a California senator in 1885.

Breaking Ground

To obtain the government's approval for the transcontinental railroad, Judah decided to accomplish as much as possible in California. This included finding investors and mapping and surveying the route. Turned down by potential investors in San Francisco, Judah suggested the idea to Sacramento businessmen in November 1860. He had better luck there. They formed the Central Pacific Railroad, incorporating on June 28, 1861. Its leaders included Leland Stanford, a storekeeper and future California governor who became the company's president; Collis Huntington, a store owner who became company vice president; and Huntington's business partner, Mark Hopkins, who became treasurer. Later, Charles Crocker, another Sacramento store owner, became part of the corporation and was in charge of railroad construction.

These merchants came to be known as the Big Four. Judah was chief engineer and on the board of directors, as was Daniel Strong, who helped Judah determine the Donner Pass as the best place for the railroad to go over the Sierra Nevada. Following the incorporation, Central Pacific's leaders sent Judah to Washington DC to persuade the federal government to give them bonds and land to help pay for the

Stanford University

Prestigious Stanford University in Palo Alto, California, was founded by Central Pacific president Leland Stanford to honor his only son, who died of typhoid fever in 1884 at age 15. Alumni include the founders of Google and Yahoo!, former National Football League stars, US Supreme Court justices, and US President Herbert Hoover.

mammoth project. The lobbying proved difficult, as the government was busy with the American Civil War, which had begun in April 1861.

Eventually Judah succeeded, in part because US President Abraham Lincoln supported the project. Additionally, because of the war, Southern members of Congress did not take part in the debate or vote on the issue, which expedited the decision-making process. On July 1, 1862, Lincoln signed the Pacific Railroad Act, which gave the Central Pacific Railroad the job of building the transcontinental railroad from Sacramento eastward.

American Civil War

The start of the transcontinental railroad project coincided with the American Civil War. The war began in April 1861 and lasted until April 1865, when Confederate General Robert E. Lee surrendered to Union General Ulysses S. Grant in Virginia.

Slavery—the ownership, buying, and selling of people—was one of the main issues that divided the two regions. The Southern economy depended on large farms called plantations that were staffed by slaves. Northern states had abolished slavery and the slave trade was abolished earlier in the nineteenth century. Lincoln and his political party, the Republican Party, opposed the expansion of slavery into new western territories. When he was elected without help from the slave states, those states seceded. This was another main cause of the Civil War—many disagreed over the rights of states to secede from the Union. When Confederate troops attacked the federal government's Fort Sumter in South Carolina, Union forces fought back. During the four-year war, approximately 620,000 soldiers died—more American deaths than in any other war. All slaves were set free after the war.

The act called for the formation of the Union
Pacific Railroad to build westward from the Missouri
River, which was close to where the existing eastern
railroads terminated.

Because of the war, the federal government had
no money to give for the project, but it did have
land. The government promised each company five
square miles (12.9 sq km) of land in alternating
sections on either side of each mile (1.6 km) of
track, or 6,400 acres (2,600 ha) of land for
each mile of railroad built. Alternating sections
meant the one-mile sections of ground owned
by the railroad companies alternated with one-
mile sections owned by the federal government.
The companies could sell the land to make money
to build the railroad. The railroad companies
also received land for railroad stations, machine
shops, and other structures as well as materials
such as wood, stone, and earth. Furthermore, the
companies received $16,000 in government bonds
for every mile of track built on flat land, $32,000
for track built on foothills, and $48,000 for each
mile built in mountains. The railroad companies
had to sell the bonds to receive money. The bonds
were low-interest loans that had to be paid back to

the government over 30 years at a cost of 6 percent interest. Additionally, the companies sold stock, or shares of ownership in their corporations.

COMMENCEMENT

Central Pacific broke ground in Sacramento on January 8, 1863, in front of a large crowd. A reporter for the *Sacramento Union* newspaper wrote, "Everybody felt happy because, after so many years of dreaming, scheming, talking and toiling, they saw with their own eyes the actual commencement of a Pacific Railroad."[1]

The Union Pacific Railroad Corporation formed nine months later, on October 29, 1863, when stockholders chose John A. Dix as president. However, Dix did not truly run the corporation. Thomas Durant, elected vice president and general manager, was in charge. He was a former doctor who became more interested in business pursuits than in work as a physician.

Principals from both railroad companies set up companies to which they awarded the railroad's construction contracts without seeking competitive bids from other firms. For the Union Pacific, it was Crédit Mobilier of America, of which Durant

Union Pacific executives, seated at table, from left: Silas Seymour, Sidney Dillon, Thomas Durant, and John Duff

was a director. For Central Pacific, it was Charles Crocker & Company, owned by the Central Pacific partner of the same name. Crocker resigned from the Central Pacific board because of the conflict of interest. By creating Crédit Mobilier and Charles Crocker & Company, the leaders of the railroad corporations created a means to profit personally from the government project. They authorized the construction companies to do the work at inflated prices and then pocketed the profits. Crédit Mobilier also purchased government bonds from Union Pacific at the price at which they were issued originally, then sold them at a profit. The public, at the time, was unaware of the underhanded manner in which this business was conducted. But the practices would later come to light.

Around the same time, Judah became unhappy with the way the four main investors in Central Pacific were running things. He went to New York to find new investors to help him buy Central Pacific from the other original investors. Unfortunately,

Abraham Lincoln

Abraham Lincoln, the sixteenth president of the United States, supported the transcontinental railroad. He had planned to ride it to California. "I have it now in purpose when the railroad is finished, to visit your wonderful state," he told an Illinois friend returning to California in 1865.[2] Lincoln never took the ride; he was assassinated before the railroad's completion.

he contracted either yellow fever or typhoid in Panama along the way and died in New York on November 2, 1863, just as the Central Pacific Railroad became reality.

Central Pacific laid the first rails on October 26, 1863, just a few days before Union Pacific formally existed. A Central Pacific locomotive called the Governor Stanford after the company president first rode those rails on November 10, 1863, before Union Pacific had even broken ground. That would not happen until Lincoln decided where the beginning of the line would be. On November 17, 1863, two days before giving the Gettysburg Address, Lincoln gave Durant a note saying he chose Council Bluffs, a town on the Missouri River and on Iowa's western boundary. But Durant built the eastern terminus in Omaha, Nebraska, on the other side of the Missouri River from Council Bluffs and the end of eastern railroad lines.

In his book *Empire Express*, David Haward Bain wrote,

> *Lincoln plainly meant the eastern terminus to be in Council Bluffs, probably—with his kind of lawyerly thoroughness—making sure that it should be Durant's responsibility to soon build and maintain a railroad bridge over the Missouri River. But Lincoln's language had enough space for interpretation in it to drive a ten-car train through it sideways. So Durant thrust the note into his pocket, took his leave of the president, and went out to announce to the world that the Union Pacific terminus would be in Omaha. Bridging the Missouri could wait.[3]*

The Union Pacific broke ground in Omaha, Nebraska, across the Missouri River from Council

Bluffs, Iowa, on December 1, 1863, during a celebration that included bands, cannons, and fireworks.

Central Pacific train service began on February 29, 1864, when 18 miles (29 km) of railroad was finished between Sacramento and Roseville in California. Still, the project did not have enough private investors. In the absence of Southern Congressmen, the leaders of the two railroad companies convinced President Lincoln and the US Congress to pass a new railroad law on July 2 that doubled the amount of ground they would receive—and sell—for each mile (1.6 km) built. This increased the grant to ten square miles (25.9 sq km) on either side of the track, or nearly 12,800 acres (5,200 ha) per mile. They also were given the rights to all resources found on that land, such as coal and iron. And the price for Union Pacific stock was reduced. Historian Maury Klein said, "The object was to induce private parties to build the road that everyone agreed must be built."[4]

Although almost everyone may have agreed the railroad must be built, as of then, it was not. But the railroad companies were about to become busier on the road to reaching that goal. ⌐

Abraham Lincoln was a lawyer before he became president of the United States. He supported the building of the transcontinental railroad.

*Chinese laborers camped near a construction train in Nevada.
Engineers lived inside railcars and laborers set up camps nearby.*

RAILROAD WORK BEGINS

he year 1865 brought both endings and beginnings in the United States. On April 3, the Confederate capital of Richmond, Virginia, fell to the Union army. Less than one week later, Confederate General Robert E. Lee surrendered to Union General Ulysses S. Grant at the Appomattox Court House. The following week, President Abraham Lincoln was shot and killed by a Confederate sympathizer. Despite this tragic event, the upheaval marked the end of war and the beginning of a peace distinguished by the nation's growth. "With an almost explosive force the industrial, financial, and transportation systems of the North were let loose," wrote historian Stephen E. Ambrose.[1] With money and people now available for peacetime pursuits, the Union Pacific and Central Pacific railroad companies quickened the pace on transcontinental railroad construction.

The end of the war meant Union and Confederate soldiers were out of work and looking for jobs. Many found employment building the transcontinental railroad. Both

The Assassination of a President

On April 14, 1865, President Abraham Lincoln was watching the comedy *Our American Cousin* at Ford's Theatre in Washington DC. During the production, John Wilkes Booth, an actor and a Confederate sympathizer, shot Lincoln. Booth had entered Lincoln's private box and shot him in the back of the head. Lincoln died the next day. Booth was fatally shot 12 days later when he was found hiding in Virginia.

Lincoln's death had a profound effect on the country. The nation mourned the loss of the president who had served during the Civil War. Lincoln's body was carried by train to his home state of Illinois. He was buried on May 4, 1865.

railroad companies employed Irish immigrants, although many more worked for Union Pacific. The Irish railroad workers had come to the United States to escape poverty in Ireland stemming from a potato famine that began in the 1840s. Some of the Irish were Civil War veterans too.

Central Pacific employed thousands of Chinese immigrants who came to California to escape famine and hardship. Hiring of the Chinese proved necessary because white people who took jobs with Central Pacific often abandoned their positions

The Great Irish Potato Famine

Many of the Irish men who worked on the transcontinental railroad came to North America in the wake of a famine in Ireland that began in 1845 and lasted six years. It was caused by a fungus that attacked Ireland's potato plants. Three million of Ireland's 8 million citizens depended solely upon the potato plant for food. One witness wrote: "In many places the wretched people were seated on the fences of their decaying gardens, wringing their hands and wailing bitterly the destruction that had left them foodless."[2] The blight led to a national crop failure, poverty, emigration, and for some, death.

An estimated 1.5 million people died, mostly from diseases stemming from deprivation rather than from starvation. Another 1 million people left Ireland because of the conditions: no food, no work, no money, and insufficient aid from England, which ruled the country at the time.

After the famine, people continued to emigrate to escape the clinging poverty. Most went to the United States; others migrated to Canada or Australia. In 1841, Ireland's population was almost 8.2 million. About 4.5 million Irish left from 1851 to 1921.

when their work brought them close to goldfields in California or silver mines in Nevada. Calls for more workers among the white community did not bring out enough workers, so the company began recruiting the Chinese. However, the Chinese faced prejudice and legal persecution in California. They were thought to be too small and weak to be effective railroad workers. Charles Crocker, Central Pacific's construction contractor, recalled that it was difficult to convince James H. Strobridge, Central Pacific's construction superintendent, to use Chinese workers. However, the Chinese workers turned out to be efficient and diligent.

WORKING ON THE RAILROAD

The white workers of Union Pacific earned three to four dollars each day. Most Central Pacific railroad workers earned $30 to $35 a month working six days a week. The Chinese, who made up the vast majority of the workforce, were paid less initially but eventually received pay raises. White, skilled laborers, such as blacksmiths and masons, could make much more—wages of as much as five dollars per day. Food was included in the white men's wages. The Chinese workers' food was shipped to them

Horses were used to pull materials as Union Pacific labor teams constructed the track.

from California. It included seafood and vegetables and was a better diet than the meat and potatoes their white counterparts ate. The Chinese also drank tea made with boiled water. They bathed themselves and washed their clothing more often than the white men. Historians believe these practices led the Chinese to be healthier on the job than the white men. The Chinese also did not drink alcohol, although some smoked opium, an addictive drug, on their day off.

All of the men worked by hand with shovels, picks, wheelbarrows, and scrapers, which were pulled by horses or oxen. They also used blasting powder. No power tools or heavy machinery were available for the job. Work was done with hand tools and dump carts pulled by horses. Each mile (1.6 km) of track they laid required approximately 350–400 iron rails and 2,500 wooden ties. Each metal rail weighed approximately 700 pounds (320 kg) and required five men to lift it. Approximately 2,260 to 2,640 wooden ties ran perpendicular to and connected the parallel rails each mile. Each of the 10,000 metal spikes was driven by hand.

Supply Situations

Finding men to do the backbreaking work was one facet of the giant project—another was acquiring supplies for it. For example, Union Pacific surveyors, who marked where the railroad line would go by putting stakes along the path, experienced a problem as they were about to cross the Great Plains. This area contained no trees

Silver Strike in Nevada

The first major silver discovery in the United States was the Comstock Lode in Virginia City, Nevada. It was uncovered in 1859 and named for the man who claimed the land where it was found. Gold was found too. From 1859 to 1882, almost $306 million worth of ore was mined from the site.

and, therefore, no wood for stakes. On August 2, 1865, the Union Pacific's team of surveyors stopped in Columbus, a village where the Loup and Platte Rivers converged in Nebraska, and cut down trees for four days so they would have supplies for the job.

Other railroad supplies were costly. Prices had increased during the Civil War and again when the railroad companies went to market. Sources vary, but from approximately 1860 to 1869, the price of iron rail more than doubled. Furthermore, the rail had to travel great distances to reach the construction sites. Rails, engines, cars, and other equipment for Central Pacific were made in the East and had to be shipped 18,000 miles (29,000 km) around the tip of South America to California. The time-consuming process was expensive and dangerous. Some locomotives and rails were shipped via the Isthmus of Panama. While that took less time, it was more expensive. Once the materials reached San Francisco by boat, they were loaded onto other boats and shipped 130 miles (210 km) through San Francisco Bay and the Sacramento River to Sacramento. Then they were loaded on railcars and brought to the workers. For Union Pacific, materials had to be brought 175 miles (280 km) up the Missouri River to Omaha. The process slowed in the winter when the river froze.

Slow Progress

By the summer of 1865, Union Pacific began laying track from Omaha. On the other side of the continent, Central Pacific had built a short rail line. Their next project was to tackle the Sierra Nevada by digging away at the granite-filled mountains for tunnels and roadbeds. "Good engineers considered the undertaking preposterous," a writer for *Van Nostrand's Eclectic Engineering Magazine* said in 1870.[3] In an area near Sacramento called Cape Horn, a flat roadway for the rails had to be cut into and curve around a steep mountain more than 1,000 feet (300 m) above the American River.

Several historians said the job was done by Chinese workers who were lowered down the mountain's

Sierra Nevada

Sierra Nevada means "snowy mountain range," and it certainly is one. It stretches 400 miles (640 km) along California's eastern region, which borders Nevada, and is about 70 miles (110 km) wide. Included in the Sierra Nevada are Lake Tahoe, Yosemite National Park, and Sequoia National Park, which is home to the world's most massive trees.

cliff face in baskets suspended by ropes. From the hanging baskets, workers drilled holes into the rock, filled the holes with blasting powder, set fuses, and scampered up the basket ropes to safety before the explosions, which blew away the rock to create the ledge the railroad needed. Others dispute the characterization. "The description of the 'Chinese Basket Drillers' are romantic but not true," wrote historian Edson T. Strobridge.[4] Strobridge contended the slope was not steep enough to have allowed hanging baskets. Furthermore, Strobridge said, had the roadwork been done in such an unusual way, newspapers reporting on the construction likely would have recorded it—and they did not. One history writer said surveyors may have been lowered by rope in the area but not workers grading the roadbed. Another said records indicate men had ropes tied around themselves for support while they cut rock from hillsides.

By the end of 1865, Union Pacific had laid only 40 miles (65 km) of track and had more than 1,000 miles (1,600 km) to go. Central Pacific was mired in the hard work within the Sierra Nevada.

Chinese workers watch a Central Pacific train in the mountains. Thousands of Chinese immigrants helped construct the transcontinental railroad.

Laying track through the Sierra Nevada Mountains was a challenge for Central Pacific.

PROGRESS MADE

s Union Pacific began major construction and moved beyond Omaha, much of the company's work happened on the relatively flat ground of the Platte River Valley in Nebraska's Great Plains. Former Union army

General Grenville Dodge came on board in spring 1866 to direct construction. He led a work crew that included many Civil War veterans. Dodge said,

> It was the best organized, best equipped and best disciplined work force I have ever seen. I used it several times as a fighting force and it took no longer to put it into fighting line than it did to form it for daily work.[1]

By the end of 1866, Dodge's crews had built almost 300 miles (480 km) of track, passing the 100th meridian. This imaginary line of longitude (100 degrees west of Greenwich, England) bisects the United States. Once Union Pacific passed that mark on October 24, 1866, the government guaranteed it the right to continue westward. Under Dodge's command, crews laid two to three miles (3.2–4.8 km) of track each day.

As the crews moved westward, temporary, portable towns moved along with them. Called Hell-on-Wheels, the towns were fairly lawless and known for gambling,

Grenville Dodge

Grenville Dodge and Abraham Lincoln shared a history that went back before the railroad building began. Dodge, the future Union Pacific chief engineer, had met the future US president in Council Bluffs, Iowa, in 1859. When Lincoln learned that Dodge was a railroad engineer, he asked Dodge what the best route was for a transcontinental railroad. Dodge suggested beginning near Council Bluffs and continuing along the Platte Valley. That was the route eventually chosen.

prostitution, drunkenness, and violence. Writer Samuel Bowles described one such town as:

> *By day disgusting, by night dangerous, almost everybody dirty, many filthy, and with the marks of lowest vice; averaging a murder a day; gambling, drinking, hurdy-gurdy dancing and the vilest of sexual commerce.*[2]

Tunneling through the Sierra Nevada

Construction had moved much more slowly for Central Pacific early on because the company came up against the Sierra Nevada. At places where the railroad company could not go over a mountain or around it, it had to go through it by creating a tunnel. Central Pacific dug 15 tunnels for the transcontinental railroad while Union Pacific dug four in the Wasatch Mountains in Utah.

While it was not easy to dig tunnels through the Sierra's granite, there were advantages to doing the work. Once a tunnel was started, the crews could work on it through the winter because they would be protected from the snow. The tunnels shielded railroad track from snow, unlike the miles of exposed track high in the mountains that required snow sheds to be built to cover the track. Tunnels also lessened the need for another difficult job: building retaining walls on mountainsides to support exposed railroads.

In fall of 1866, Central Pacific workers worked feverishly to start the mountain tunnels before the snow came. They worked in three shifts around the clock so work could continue in the tunnels during the winter. John R. Gilliss, a Central Pacific engineer, explained the pace in an 1870 article he wrote that was published in *Van Nostrand's Eclectic Engineering Magazine*:

> As an illustration of the hurry, I may mention walking two miles over the hills after dark, and staking out the east end of [Tunnel] No. 12 by the light of a bonfire; at 9 o'clock the men were at work. [3]

To dig a tunnel, workers drove iron drills into the rock with sledgehammers to make holes eight to 12 inches (20–30 cm) deep. After making a few of those holes, they filled each hole with explosive powder and a fuse. They lit the fuses and ran for cover. After the powder exploded and the smoke cleared, they dug out and carted away the rubble,

Black Powder

Central Pacific used up to 500 kegs of black powder each day during the height of tunnel construction in the Sierra Nevada. A keg held 25 pounds (11 kg), which meant the railroad used 12,500 pounds (5,700 kg) of it daily during that period.

Summit Tunnel

dumping it over the side of the mountain. It took
one day to make less than two feet (.6 m) of progress.
It required a lot of explosive black powder, also
known as black gunpowder. At the peak of railroad
construction through the mountains, 500 kegs of
black powder were used each day.

Tunnel No. 6 was the most difficult and longest tunnel to dig at 1,659 feet (506 m) long. It was also known as the Summit Tunnel because it was 7,000 feet (2,100 m) high and near the mountain summit. To begin that tunnel, Central Pacific sunk a shaft through the mountain to where the middle of the tunnel would be. Crews worked from the inside of the mountain outwardly while other crews dug inwardly from each end of the tunnel. The mountain granite was so hard it took 85 days just to dig a shaft 73 feet (22 m) long. Each day, an average of ten inches (25.4 cm) was dug. In February 1867, Central Pacific began using nitroglycerin, a newly invented explosive compound that was more powerful than black powder. The use of nitroglycerin almost doubled the speed of tunneling through the mountains, although Central Pacific eventually abandoned the compound because of its tendency to blow up unexpectedly.

SIERRAS IN THE SNOW

In the winter of 1866–1867, the mountain tunnels had all been started and the tunnel crews were working underground protected from the weather. Working inside the tunnels was a great benefit as there were 44 snowstorms that winter in the Sierra Nevada. Gilliss, Central Pacific's engineer, noted one storm in particular that began at 2:00 p.m. on February 18, 1867, and ended at 10:00 p.m. on February 22. In that time, six feet (1.8 m) of snow fell. Five days later, snow began falling again and did not stop until March 2. The total accumulation was ten feet (3 m).

The weather did not cause the work to stop. Tunnels were cut through the snow so supplies could come in and material dug from the middle of the mountains could

Nitroglycerin

When chemist Ascanio Sobrero created the explosive compound nitroglycerin in 1864, he worried so much about the unstable product's potential for destruction that he destroyed his notes. Nonetheless, it still was manufactured. Central Pacific was eager to try it in the Sierra Nevada where the railroad company was making slow progress blowing away granite with black gunpowder. In 1866, Central Pacific received part of a San Francisco shipment of the product and tested it. Another part of the shipment began leaking on a San Francisco wharf and was taken to an office building in town. Unfortunately, employees decided to open the unmarked crate to see what was inside. The crate exploded, leveling that building and others around it and killing 15 people. Soon after, six Central Pacific workers were killed when a nitroglycerin sample exploded unexpectedly. The explosions led California to confiscate nitroglycerin and ban its transport.

Central Pacific still wanted it, however, because it blew up rock a lot better than blasting powder. The company solved the problem by hiring British chemist James Howden to make nitroglycerin on location in the mountains where it was to be used.

be hauled out. In one case, Gilliss reported that a snow tunnel was cut through a snowdrift on the side of a mountain to join the two entrances of a mountain tunnel under construction. Windows were cut into the snow for light and to discard the material dug out of the mountain. The snow tunnel even had a flight of snow stairs that led down to a blacksmith's shop, buried still deeper in the snow.

But the mountain snow was dangerous, and there were casualties for the rail workers. One snowslide carried away 20 workers. Gilliss wrote that "avalanches [would] sweep over the shanties of the laborers."[4] Surveyor J. O. Wilder reported snow so deep at his camp it had to be shoveled from rooftops and kept people from entering and leaving. "Had it lasted one week longer we would have been compelled to eat horse meat," Wilder said.[5]

Snow Saga

Due to the amount of snowfall in the Sierra Nevada, half of the 10,000 people working there during the winter of 1866–1867 had the job of shoveling snow. In addition, Central Pacific eventually had to build 37 miles (60 km) of snow sheds to protect track that did not go through mountain tunnels.

STRIKE

While in the Sierra Nevada, the Chinese workers went on strike on June 25, 1867, to seek higher wages. Some other workers were making approximately $60–$100 per month, depending on the work they did, but the Chinese were making $30 per month. The railroad company offered $35 per month, but the Chinese wanted $40. Central Pacific cut off the Chinese workers' food and supplies, threatened them with replacement and loss of pay for a month, and brought in armed men for intimidation. After one week of striking, the Chinese went back to work at the $35 per month wage.

The Chinese and the rest of the Central Pacific crew finished the Summit Tunnel by the end of 1867. Tracks now connected all of the tunnels in the Sierra Nevada. Crews also had been laying track east of the mountains while work continued

Grudging Respect

Central Pacific construction chief Charles Crocker did not give in to Chinese demands during their work stoppage, but he did express a bit of respect: "If there had been that number of whites in a strike, there would have been murder, drunkenness and disorder. . . . But with the Chinese, it was just like Sunday. . . . No violence was perpetrated along the whole line."[6]

on the tunnels, so Central Pacific track crossed the state line into Nevada by the end of 1867 as well. On the other side, Union Pacific had finished laying another 240 miles (390 km) of track.

USE BEFORE COMPLETION

As the work progressed, newspapers and magazines updated readers with the developments. The project was portrayed early on as a great and monumental endeavor. In a December 1867 article, the *Atlantic Monthly* called the Pacific Railroad "the world's great highway" for commerce between East and West. The article also claimed that the project's significance extended beyond trade. It would connect a broken nation and hasten the development of the country: "It will populate the West in a few years; and along its lines will spring up a hundred cities, which will advance in the swift march of national progress."[7]

Towns and cities already were springing up along the line. And as the building continued, trains carried passengers on the portions of rail that had been completed. In the early years of construction, travel was possible within California on the Central Pacific line and within Nebraska on the Union

Pacific line. Near the end of construction, when more rail line was operational, settlers would take the Union Pacific line as far west as it would go, then hire a stagecoach to take them to where Central Pacific train service was available. From that point on, they could ride a Central Pacific train to California. The newspapers were right: the railway would help settlers populate the vast nation.

Settlers were not the only ones to avail themselves of this convenience. Historian Stephen Ambrose reported that a US Army regiment ordered to report to San Francisco took Union Pacific in April 1869 to Corinne. This small Utah town had been founded on the Union Pacific line only a month earlier. The regiment then marched for two days to where Central Pacific's line began and boarded a Central Pacific train for the trip to the coast. The trip from Omaha, Nebraska, to Sacramento, California, took about a week. "No American army unit had ever before moved so fast or so far for less money or at such ease," Ambrose wrote.[8]

*As the railroad progressed across the Great Plains, small towns
and railroad stations sprang up along the way.*

An illustration of Cheyenne Indians attacking railroad workers appeared in *Harper's Weekly* in 1867.

LAND BATTLES AND CONTINUING THE WORK

As 1867 turned into 1868, the Union Pacific's line moved from Nebraska into Wyoming. The railroad experienced the most conflict with American Indians in the Great Plains.

AMERICAN INDIANS AND THE RAILROAD

The Great Plains, the flat grasslands in the center of the United States, was home to various American-Indian tribes who had lived there for many generations. The transcontinental railroad cleaved the region and the massive buffalo herd that provided sustenance to many American Indians. It also brought construction crews and settlers in greater numbers than wagon trains and stagecoaches had brought previously. The railroad—and the men who came with it—drastically affected the American Indians' ways of life. Some American-Indian tribes, such as the Pawnee, accepted the new presence. They worked with the US Army to protect railroad construction crews from attack by other American Indians. Other tribes, such as the Cheyenne and the Sioux, did not like the encroachment of the railroad project and took action against it. Historians list a number of episodes in which American Indians attacked trains, tracks, and train stations, killing railroad employees and train passengers. The US Army established

Great Plains

The Great Plains includes broad expanses of relatively flat grassland in Colorado, Kansas, Montana, Nebraska, New Mexico, North Dakota, Oklahoma, South Dakota, Texas, and Wyoming as well as Alberta, Manitoba, and Saskatchewan in Canada. It is known for cattle and sheep herding and farming wheat and other grain crops.

American Bison

Also called a buffalo, the American bison is a large, hairy mammal that once was the most abundant grazing animal in North America. Calves weigh about 65 pounds (29 kg) at birth. Cows grow to about 1,100 pounds (500 kg). Bulls grow to approximately 2,000 pounds (900 kg). The animals can live up to 40 years in captivity.

American Indians who hunted bison did so for more than just meat. Bison horns could be used as cups, toys, spoons, or decoration. Hides were used for blankets, shelter, or clothing. Other parts of the animals became instruments or weapons. Bison largely defined the lives of Plains Indians, but these animals were overhunted by white people. The mass decrease in bison populations had devastating effects on the American Indians who depended on the animals for survival.

a number of forts along the railroad route in Nebraska, Colorado, and Wyoming to protect the railroad. The army also attacked and killed American Indians.

The conflicts interfered with construction. As Union Pacific's chief engineer, Grenville Dodge, saw things, ending the conflict meant ridding the area of the native peoples. "We've got to clean the damn Indians out, or give up building the Union Pacific Railroad," Dodge said.[1]

What Dodge proposed is essentially what happened. Railroad workers and pioneers killed buffalo in great numbers, which impacted the American Indians because they relied on buffalo for food and other uses. By the early 1880s, the buffalo herds were largely wiped out.

The federal government further changed the American Indians' ways of living by moving them from the land where they had lived freely for generations. But this movement was not without resistance, and fights broke out between the US Army and American-Indian tribes. During the 1860s, a series of conflicts called the Plains Wars ensued. This included the Washita River Massacre in which officer George Armstrong Custer and US soldiers killed more than 100 Cheyenne. In 1876, the Cheyenne and the Sioux attacked Custer and his men at the Battle of the Little Bighorn. Custer and all of his men were killed.

By the 1880s, most American Indians were placed on smaller reservations out of the way of easterners moving in to settle the West. Among those instrumental in moving the American Indians onto reservations was US Army General William Tecumseh Sherman, who had played a large role in securing the Union victory in the Civil War. Sherman was named after an American Indian named Tecumseh who had fought against American encroachment in the early 1800s and had sided with the British against the United States in the War of 1812.

Union Pacific Heads into the West

On April 16, 1868, Union Pacific placed rails atop Sherman Summit, Wyoming, the highest point on the line at 8,200 feet (2,500 m). Durant not only laid the final rail, he also sent a telegram to Stanford to brag about the accomplishment.

In May 1868, Brigham Young was the president of the Church of Jesus Christ of Latter-Day Saints, otherwise known as the Mormon Church. Young and many Mormons had settled in Utah. The church received a $2 million Union Pacific contract to grade, or make level, the ground for the railroad from the Wyoming-Utah

General William Tecumseh Sherman and the American Indians

During the Civil War, General William Tecumseh Sherman captured two important cities in Georgia, Atlanta and Savannah, from the Confederacy. He is blamed for the burning of Atlanta. After the war, he was the US Army commander in charge of the portion of the country that stretched from the Mississippi River west to the Rocky Mountains. Part of that job involved protecting the transcontinental railroad from American Indians attacking workers because it went through their territory.

Sherman was a member of the commissions that negotiated treaties with American-Indian tribes. These treaties led to those tribes moving onto reservations. Sherman advocated the policy and once said American Indians not on reservations "are hostile and will remain so until killed off."[2] He became the US Army's general commander in 1869. Under his command, the military took action against the American Indians on the Great Plains. Some American Indians, including a group of Chiricahua Apache led by Geronimo, resisted resettlement numerous times. Later in his life, some considered Sherman a good candidate for US president. Sherman did not want the job, saying, "If nominated, I will not run. If elected, I will not serve."[3]

border to the Great Salt Lake in Utah. The workers were members of the Latter-Day Saints church.

CENTRAL PACIFIC MOVES OUT OF CALIFORNIA

Central Pacific finished its work in California, connecting the rail lines in the Sierra Nevada with track built to the east of the range. On May 4, 1868, the rails reached Lake's Crossing in Nevada. Crocker renamed the town Reno to honor Jesse Lee Reno, a general killed in the Civil War. The first passenger train crossed the Sierra and arrived in Reno on June 18, 1868.

By 1868, Central Pacific had 51 freight and passenger locomotives riding on the new track. But with everything they had achieved, there was still a problem. It was a single track, so accidents were a threat, especially in situations where visibility was poor, such as around curves. It was not easy to slow or stop a train. Brakemen stationed on the roof of the train had to operate each railcar's brakes

Mormon Church

Much of Utah's history involves settlements established by members of the Mormon Church. The religion was founded in New York in 1830 by Joseph Smith Jr. After Smith's death in 1844, Brigham Young brought a large group of Mormons to the West in the 1840s, seeking religious freedom. They settled in the Great Salt Lake region and spread out from there. Today, Utah is home to Brigham Young University and the Salt Lake Temple.

separately. They ran along the roof, manually activated a brake, then leapt to the next car, ran to its brake, and repeated the process until the two brakemen met at the middle of the train. It could take a half mile (.8 km) for a train to come to a full stop.

Once in Nevada, the hardest days of construction were behind Central Pacific. It began building on the relatively flat desert. Instead of measuring daily progress by inches as it had in the Sierra Nevada, it was measuring it by as many as three to four miles (4.8–6.4 km) per day. However, the company learned it would not have much luck supplying its construction needs from the land itself. Surveyor Lewis Clement remarked:

> There was not a tree that would make a board on over 500 miles of the route, no satisfactory quality of building stone. The country offered nothing.[4]

COMPETITION

The two companies began competing to arrive at the finish line in Utah before the other. The company that arrived first at Ogden and the established Mormon communities of Utah's Great

A Union Pacific construction crew in 1867

Salt Lake could benefit economically by establishing a depot there. That depot would receive the railroad business into and out of that area, including trade to the West, because no other settlements existed between the Mormon communities and Sacramento. The competition and the fact that the railroad companies were paid according to quantity—how many miles of railroad were built, rather than according to the quality of construction—meant that quality suffered for the sake of quantity during the race to the finish. One example was the Granite Canyon Fill in Wyoming where a depression was filled to make the ground more level for the rails. It was supposed to be 14 feet (4.3 m) wide, but at places it was only the width of an 8-foot- (2.4-m-) long railroad tie, if that. "In several places I saw ends of the ties projecting over the embankment," wrote Isaac N. Morris, a government inspector.[5]

Until mid-1868, the most track laid by either company was four miles (6.4 km) in a single day. That record was broken by Union Pacific, which laid four and one-half miles (7.2 km) of track in one day. Central Pacific responded by laying six miles (9.7 km) of track one day in Nevada. It was Union Pacific's turn, and they put down seven and one-half miles (12.1 km) in one 15-hour day. The accomplishment led Durant to bet Crocker $10,000 that the record could not be bested. Only time would tell if the record would stand.

Central Pacific finished another 305 miles (490 km) of track by the end of 1868. By the end of the same year, Union Pacific had laid rails as far as Evanston, Wyoming, near the Utah border. Almost 1,000 miles (1,600 km) of track had been laid from Omaha westward since July 1865.

The building of the transcontinental railroad had a profound
effect on the lives of American Indians.

Central Pacific workers stand on a trestle near Promontory, Utah, in 1868.

THE FINAL STRETCH

U nion Pacific and Central Pacific raced each other to the finish line in Utah. Central Pacific, which spent so much time mired in the Sierra Nevada, worried Union Pacific would arrive first.

"I believe they will beat us nearly to the
state line," said Strobridge, Central Pacific's
superintendent of construction, referring to
the state line between Nevada and Utah during a
conversation with Crocker.[1]

"We have got to beat them," Crocker replied.[2]
Central Pacific crossed the Nevada state line
into Utah before Union Pacific met them there.
However, by the spring of 1869, Union Pacific
reached Ogden, Utah, first, seemingly collecting for
itself the lucrative business in the region's Mormon
communities and its trade with the West.

Where Is the Finish Line?

In April, Union Pacific was going up the east
side of the Promontory Mountains and Central
Pacific was going up the west side. The rail-laying
teams were approximately 50 miles (80 km) apart.
The grading teams, which worked far ahead of
the rail layers, already had passed each other,
missing the connection. Union Pacific graded to
some extent almost 170 miles (270 km) west of
Promontory Summit while Central Pacific had gone
past Promontory Summit to the east. The situation
meant the two companies built two railroad grades

parallel to each other for about 200 miles (320 km) when only one grade was needed.

Until that time, everyone knew the finish line was in Utah—but where exactly in Utah would it be? To end the wastefulness, the federal government told representatives from the two railroad companies to determine where the finish would be. The representatives chose Promontory Summit, north of the Great Salt Lake. The compromise was that Union Pacific would build a railroad from Ogden to the joining place but then sell it to Central Pacific for $4 million, a price that was later reduced. On April 10, 1869, a federal law established Promontory Summit as the place where the two railroads would join.

A Record Day

To that point, Union Pacific held the record for placing the most track in one day—nearly eight miles (12.9 km). Crocker wanted to break that by laying ten miles (16.1 km) of

Too Close for Comfort

The two railroad companies not only passed each other in Utah, they sometimes worked within view of each other. "At one point they are probably within two hundred feet of us," Central Pacific president Leland Stanford said. "From Bear River to the Promontory, we are so close that the U.P. cross us twice. In other areas their line occasionally runs within a few feet!"[3]

Charles Crocker was a businessman and a politician before joining Central Pacific.

track in one day. He chose a day at the end of April 1869, when Union Pacific was closer than ten miles to the finish line. Crocker said, "We must not beat them until we get so close together that there is not enough room for them to turn around and outdo me."[4]

Beat Union Pacific is just what Central Pacific did on April 28, 1869. Three thousand workers, more than 100 horses, and many mule teams were part of the effort. Each worker had a specific job to do and then moved on to do it again farther forward on the line. Two miles' (3.2 km) worth of rails was dumped at a time. Workers carried the rails to where they were needed. Others put them into place. Still other workers drove the spikes, each driving a spike into a particular spot on a rail, and then moving forward to drive a spike in the same place in the next rail. Levelers and fillers raised ties and shoveled dirt underneath them when necessary—and kept moving. Crocker offered to relieve the tracklayers with a reserve team but they refused.

A soldier who watched the workers described the progress as about the pace his horse could walk. "I never saw such organization as that; it was just like an army marching over the ground and leaving a track built behind them," the soldier said.[5]

Two million pounds (907,000 kg) of iron rail were laid

The Big Fill

One of the last big jobs undertaken by Central Pacific in 1869 was filling a ravine that was 500 feet (150 m) wide and up to 70 feet (21 m) deep in places to accommodate track. It took two months and 10,000 cubic yards (7,650 cu m) of dirt to finish the job. The track remained in use until 1942.

that day. In addition, more than 84,500 spikes were driven, and 14,088 nuts and bolts were put through 3,522 metal plates that joined abutting rails. At the end of the day, the total distance of track laid was 10.01 miles (16.11 km). Later, Union Pacific officials quibbled a bit about the feat because it was done without leaving Union Pacific room to retaliate.

THE END OF THE LINE

Central Pacific had built 690 miles (1,110 km) eastward from Sacramento, and Union Pacific built 1,086 miles (1,748 km) westward from Omaha. The date set for joining Central Pacific's railroad with Union Pacific's

Promontory Summit

While Promontory Summit was the site of the historic joining of the transcontinental railroad, only a temporary city existed there from May until December 1869 when the permanent terminus was established in Ogden. Trains continued to go through the area until the early twentieth-century construction of the 102-mile (164-km) Lucin Cutoff, which created a more direct route to Ogden.

Today, the Golden Spike National Historic Site operates on the spot. It became part of the US National Park system in 1965. In 1969, an estimated 28,000 people traveled to the site to celebrate the 100-year anniversary of the joining ceremony. In 1979, the site added two fully functional, life-size replicas of the steam engines that met that day: the Jupiter and the No. 119. During the summer months, visitors can see reenactments of the ceremony that took place on May 10, 1869. The visitor center also screens train-related films regularly, including *The Great Train Robbery*. Made in 1903, this 11-minute production was the first feature film comprised of edited clips pieced together instead of one long scene.

Union Pacific workers named One Thousand Mile Tree to mark their one-thousandth mile of track laid west from Omaha, Nebraska, in 1869.

railroad at Promontory Summit was Saturday, May 8, 1869. Celebrations were planned in San Francisco, Sacramento, Philadelphia, Chicago, New York, and elsewhere in the country. They also were planned for Promontory Summit. Officials from both companies planned to arrive for the ceremony by riding trains along the new tracks.

On May 6, 1869, the train carrying Union Pacific officials, including leader Thomas Durant, was nearing Wyoming's border with Utah when gunfire stopped the train in its tracks. Railroad ties were piled on the rails. An unexpected mob of several hundred Union Pacific laborers uncoupled the Pullman Palace car carrying the railroad company executives. Due to poor accounting practices and a shortage of cash, these workers had not been paid in months. With the railroad car and the executives in it under their control, the workers demanded the company officials pay them what they were owed—a sum that exceeded $200,000. Durant was taken to a telegraph station to ask other company officials for the money, which was supplied the next day.

This was not the only delay the Union Pacific officials faced on their trip west. In Utah, flooding washed out supports for a railroad bridge over the Weber River. Determining the damaged bridge would not accept the heavy weight of the engine, the engineer gave the lighter passenger cars a push to go over the bridge and another locomotive—No. 119—was sent to pull them the rest of the way. Because of the problems, the

Closing Up Shop

As construction of the transcontinental railroad wound down in May 1869, Union Pacific engineer Grenville Dodge likened the situation to the end of the Civil War four years earlier. He had served in the Union army during the war. "Closing the accounts is like the close of the Rebellion," he said.[6]

ceremony planned for the joining of the railroad was postponed from Saturday, May 8, to Monday, May 10.

The special train carrying Stanford also experienced trouble on its way to Promontory. Woodcutters working on a mountainside, unaware that the Stanford train was coming, cut down a tree that blocked the tracks. The engine crashed into it and was damaged. Stanford's cars then were coupled to a regular passenger train, pulled by the Jupiter engine, for the remainder of the journey. It arrived on May 7 and its passengers learned the Union Pacific delay meant that the marriage of the two companies' tracks could not happen before May 10. Stanford's train went on a small excursion and returned on May 9. The next day, with participants, spectators, and reporters on hand, the Union Pacific train arrived and the two portions of the transcontinental railroad were joined.

Golden Spike Ceremony at Promontory in May 1869

A group reenacts the celebration after the driving of the final spike at the Golden Spike National Historic Site in May 2000.

THE EFFECTS OF
THE RAILROAD

*W*ithin days of Stanford driving the golden spikes at Promontory Summit, a passenger could travel from New York to California in seven days—including stops. This saved weeks over the several months it took before the transcontinental railroad existed. As many as 150,000 people took advantage of this convenience in the first year. A third-class ticket cost approximately $70 (approximately $1,100 today) and meant making the trip sitting on a bench. A first-class ticket cost approximately $150 (approximately $2,400 today), which allowed the ticket holder to sleep in a Pullman car. Before the rail option was available, it cost more than $1,000 (almost $16,000 today) to travel from the East Coast by ship to either the Isthmus of Panama or around Cape Horn in South America and then up the West Coast. Taking the route by stagecoach cost about $300.

The cost of shipping freight and mail also dropped dramatically as did the amount of time it took for those shipments to reach their destinations. Initially, short lines owned by different companies made shipping goods slow and cumbersome. Many stops were required and goods from one line had to be unloaded onto another line to continue shipment. Trunk lines, which were longer and united lines spanning great distances, helped to smooth this process.

Additionally, the telegraph lines strung along the railroad allowed information to move from coast to coast as fast as it could be typed. The ability to move goods and information around the country quickly and cheaply "made modern America possible," asserted historian Stephen Ambrose.[1] It allowed not only for a continent-wide economy wherein people and goods could go virtually anywhere but also a continent-wide culture in which books, magazines, and entertainment could be readily available to many locations more easily. The impact was revolutionary for the growing nation.

Repair Needed

Before a lot of transcontinental travel could take place, however, much of the railroad had to be repaired or replaced. Because the government paid Union Pacific and Central Pacific in land and loans for each mile (1.6 km) of railroad they made, quantity and speed were rewarded at the expense of

Payback

The federal government eventually was repaid for the almost $65 million in loans it made to construct the transcontinental railroad. By the end of the nineteenth century, almost $168 million was repaid in principal, which is the original amount of the loan, and in interest, which is the price paid for borrowing money.

quality. Deficiencies were caused by inexpensive supplies used to increase profits. In addition, railroad technology was fairly new. All of these factors resulted in a product that did not always work well. Historian Richard White explained,

> Despite all the effort that went into them, these lines were poorly constructed. Railroad technology remained primitive. Iron rails rusted quickly, and untreated wooden ties rotted between them. Engineers made curves too sharp, and workers laid ballast improperly so that the roadbeds collapsed. . . . By the time the Union Pacific made its juncture with the Central Pacific, the line already needed nearly 7 million dollars' worth of repairs, and the worst sections of its tracks could barely support a locomotive. [2]

Bridge over the Missouri

Although a railroad bridge spanning the Missouri River did not open until 1873, rail traffic still managed to travel between Iowa and Nebraska. Trains rode on temporary tracks across the frozen water in the winter. When the ice melted, ferries carried passengers and cargo from one side to the other.

Furthermore, the rail line did not truly connect the East Coast to the West Coast yet. It was not until November 1869 that the railroad reached from Sacramento to the San Francisco Bay. In addition, the rails did not yet span the Missouri River between Council Bluffs, Iowa, and Omaha, Nebraska. A $2.9 million railroad bridge opened in March 1873.

SCANDAL

As the bridge across the Missouri River was under construction, scandal engulfed the railroad project. The *New York Sun* newspaper ran a story on September 4, 1872, that finally made the public aware of how railroad executives handled the transcontinental railroad's financing. It described how Crédit Mobilier, the company set up by Union Pacific executives to build the railroad, bribed congressmen to receive favorable government treatment. The story also exposed how railroad executives became rich from government railroad funding.

Congress held hearings on the matter. Union Pacific directors had a difficult time explaining why their company was almost broke in spite of all the government financing it had received. Besides exposing the details of the railroad company's business practices, the hearings led to the censure of a few congressmen who allegedly distributed Crédit Mobilier stock to colleagues. This included Oakes Ames, a member of the House of Representatives from Massachusetts. Central Pacific also was investigated but its financial books had burned, either deliberately or accidentally, so its directors faced no punishment.

WESTERN SETTLEMENT

The railroad scandal did not hinder railroad use or expansion. New rail lines grew in every direction, scattering settlers to

Rail Travel in the United States Today

The Union Pacific Railroad Corporation, established in the 1860s to build the transcontinental railroad, continues to exist today. It is a huge operation that resulted from numerous mergers. This includes a merger in the 1990s with the Southern Pacific Railroad, which was a descendant of the Central Pacific Railroad. Today the Union Pacific Railroad includes 32,100 miles (51,700 km) of railroad routes and employs almost 42,000 people.

Today, most rail use in the United States is for freight. Federally subsidized Amtrak is the only company that moves people between US metropolitan areas, although some of those areas have public transportation systems with rail lines that are linked.

Some government and special interest groups encourage train use as a way to reduce the use of automobiles. Greater use of public transportation systems could reduce the use of fossil fuels such as petroleum-derived gasoline and diesel, which cause pollution and are in dwindling supply. Some in the federal government, including US President Barack Obama, believe more people will use the railroads if high-speed trains—those going faster than 155 miles per hour (250 km/h)—are built. High-speed trains could compete with airlines for customers. In Europe, high-speed trains are frequently used for travel within or between large cities.

No Road to Asia

Early advocates of the transcontinental railroad expected it to make North America the middle-man for trade between Asia and Europe. Before 1869, travel between the continents required travel around Africa. However, the Suez Canal in Egypt opened in 1869. The artificial waterway allows water travel between Europe and Asia without navigation around Africa.

populate the middle of the continent. More than 7,000 cities and towns west of the Missouri River began as Union Pacific depots and water stops. Some little towns and cities grew big, such as Omaha.

One city that benefited from the railroad was Ogden, Utah, which replaced Promontory Summit as the terminus for both railroads approximately six months after the joining ceremony. Union Pacific, which built the line from Promontory Summit to Ogden, sold it to Central Pacific for approximately $2.9 million as part of a deal struck when Promontory Summit was chosen as the joining point. With the change, Promontory Summit became a whistle-stop and was left virtually desolate once again. Later, it was bypassed by the railroad altogether.

Citizens applied political pressure to have Promontory Summit memorialized for its place in US history. Today, the Golden Spike National Historic Site operates there under the protection of the National Park Service.

Union Pacific workers remove old track to make room for a high-speed rail in Illinois in September 2010.

Decline of the American Indians

The railroad's influence on the growth of settlements and cities west of the Mississippi River greatly affected the lives and cultures of the American Indians who lived there. The herds of bison, upon which many American Indians relied for food, were displaced by the railroad. The animals became overhunted by railroad passengers, soldiers, and white hunters to the point of extinction. Several historians have stated that millions of bison were killed in just a few decades following the construction of the railroad, leaving approximately 1,000 roaming freely. This forced the American Indians to rely on white Americans for their food supply. That made them poorer because they had to pay for food when they had previously hunted it without cost. They also lost the many parts of their culture associated with hunting.

Furthermore, the federal government forced American Indians onto reservations to make way for railroads and the resulting settlement by whites. Throughout the nineteenth century, numerous battles ensued between the US Army and American-Indian tribes as settlers pushed westward. As the American Indians' food supply began to wane, most conceded to reservation life. But the effects of westward expansion had greatly impacted their populations. Millions of American Indians lived on the American continent when Englishmen sailed into Virginia in the early 1600s. By the late nineteenth century, the US American-Indian population was approximately 250,000. This massive population decline was greatly caused by the introduction of diseases from Europe, such as smallpox, influenza, and measles. However, the destruction of American-Indian ways of life and encroachment upon their lands played large parts in the decline of these native populations.

THE UNITED STATES GROWS WITH THE RAILROAD

While the population of American Indians declined, the US population increased overall. In 1870, America had slightly more than 38 million citizens according to the US Census. By 1900, that number had reached 76 million. The population in California tripled from 560,247 in 1870 to almost 1.5 million by 1900.

During the years of California's rapid growth, no doubt many new residents of California—and the nation—engaged in train travel. It took approximately 40 years from the time the first railroad opened

Time Zones

One problem that had to be solved following the completion of the transcontinental railroad was train scheduling. This was complicated because time was not standardized. In 1884, at a convention attended by 19 nations in Washington DC, the world was divided into 24 time zones. Four time zones cover the continental United States: Eastern, Standard, Mountain, and Pacific.

in the United States in 1830 for a railroad to span the continent. But the labor and persistence of the workers who built the transcontinental railroad would have lasting effects. In uniting the eastern and western United States, those who labored to build the railroad not only provided a means of transportation—they connected a growing nation and forever changed the face of a continent.

*Built from 1863 to 1869, the transcontinental railroad
revolutionized travel in the United States.*

TIMELINE

1853	1861	1862
On March 3, Congress directs Jefferson Davis to find a route for a railroad to reach from the Mississippi River to the Pacific Ocean.	The Central Pacific Railroad formally incorporates on June 28.	On July 1, President Abraham Lincoln signs the Pacific Railroad Act allowing for the building of a transcontinental railroad.

1863	1863	1863
A locomotive rides the newly installed Central Pacific rails for the first time on November 10.	On November 17, Lincoln directs Union Pacific to build its eastern terminus near Council Bluffs, Iowa.	Union Pacific breaks ground in Omaha, Nebraska, on December 1.

1863	1863	1863
On January 8, Central Pacific breaks ground on the project with a ceremony in Sacramento, California.	The first rails are laid for Central Pacific's portion of the railroad on October 26.	The Union Pacific Railroad Corporation forms on October 29.

1864	1864	1865
Central Pacific finishes 18 miles (29 km) of railroad on February 29; train service begins on the Central Pacific line.	On July 2, the Pacific Railroad Act of 1864 doubles the amount of land granted to each railroad company for each mile of railroad built.	On April 15, Abraham Lincoln dies after being shot the previous night by John Wilkes Booth.

TIMELINE

1865	1865	1866
Central Pacific begins drilling tunnels through the Sierra Nevada Mountains in the summer.	Union Pacific spikes its first rails in Omaha, Nebraska, on July 10.	On October 24, Union Pacific passes the 100th meridian; the government guarantees it the right to continue building westward.

1868	1868	1869
On April 16, Union Pacific reaches Sherman Summit in the Rocky Mountains, the highest point on the transcontinental railroad.	On June 18, a Central Pacific passenger train crosses the Sierra Nevada and goes to Reno, Nevada, for the first time.	On April 10, federal law establishes Promontory Summit, Utah, as the point for the Union Pacific and Central Pacific railroads to meet.

1867

In February, Central Pacific begins making nitroglycerin on site for blasting tunnels in the Sierra Nevada.

1867

Central Pacific's Chinese workers go on strike on June 25. It lasts one week.

1867

On August 28, Central Pacific blasts through the Summit Tunnel, the longest tunnel in the Sierra Nevada.

1869

On April 28, Central Pacific railroad workers set a record by laying more than ten miles (16.1 km) of rail in one day in Utah.

1869

On May 6, rail workers stop the train carrying Union Pacific executives to the joining ceremony, demanding back pay.

1869

On May 10, the Union Pacific Railroad and the Central Pacific Railroad join at Promontory Summit, Utah.

Essential Facts

Date of Event

January 8, 1863—May 10, 1869

Place of Event

From Sacramento, California, eastward and from Omaha, Nebraska, westward. The two railroads met in Promontory, Utah.

Key Players

❖ Asa Whitney
❖ Theodore Judah
❖ Daniel Strong
❖ Leland Stanford
❖ Charles Crocker
❖ Collis Huntington
❖ Mark Hopkins
❖ James Strobridge
❖ Abraham Lincoln
❖ Grenville Dodge
❖ Thomas Durant

Highlights of Event

❖ In February 1832, an editorial in a Michigan newspaper called for the building of a transcontinental railroad.

❖ In March 1853, Jefferson Davis began work searching for a route for a railroad from the Mississippi River to the Pacific Ocean.

❖ On July 1, 1862, President Abraham Lincoln signed the Pacific Railroad Act. This allowed Central Pacific to build eastward from Sacramento and Union Pacific to build westward from Omaha.

❖ Central Pacific broke ground on January 8, 1863, in Sacramento. Union Pacific broke ground on December 1, 1863, in Omaha.

❖ Executives from the Central Pacific Railroad Company arrived by train at the meeting site in Promontory, Utah, on May 9, 1869. Executives from the Union Pacific Railroad Company arrived by train at the meeting site the morning of May 10, 1869.

❖ Railroad gangs from the two companies placed the last rails and the last tie. Central Pacific president Leland Stanford and Union Pacific vice president Thomas Durant drove in ceremonial spikes.

❖ Within days, paying customers traveled from New York to California via the rail line.

Quote

"Little you realize what you have done. You have this day changed the path of commerce and finance of the whole world."—*Central Pacific official James Campbell, during a speech at Promontory celebrating the joining of the railroad*

Glossary

ballast
Coarse rock or gravel that forms the bed for railroads.

bond
A way to borrow money in which one party sells a debt certificate that guarantees the buyer will repay the amount on the certificate plus interest or a percentage of the original amount borrowed by a specific date.

bribe
Something of value, such as money or a favor, offered or given to a powerful person, such as a politician, to influence that person to make decisions favorable to the person offering the item of value.

censure
A formal judgment of disapproval.

deadlock
A stalemate that occurs when members of a jury cannot agree upon a verdict.

economy
Activities related to the making, delivery, buying, and selling of products and services in a region.

editorial
An article in a publication expressing the opinion of the editors or publishers.

foothills
Hills near the bottom of a mountain or mountain range.

incorporation
The creation of a business recognized by the state as a legal entity separate from its owners.

infirm
Physically weak because of age or illness.

investors
> People who commit their money or resources to a venture with the hope that the venture will earn enough money to repay the original commitment as well as earn a profit.

locomotive
> A self-propelled vehicle used for pushing or pulling cars carrying freight or passengers on railroad tracks.

mason
> Someone who lays stone or brick.

navigation
> Method of guiding a vehicle, usually a ship, aircraft, or spacecraft, from one place to another.

prospectors
> People who search for mineral deposits or oil in an area.

secede
> To withdraw from membership in a group.

surveying
> Determining the boundaries and elevation for a railroad.

terminus
> The end of a transportation line.

veterans
> People who have served in the armed forces.

whistle-stop
> A town or a train station at which the train only stops if a passenger signals it to do so.

ADDITIONAL RESOURCES

SELECTED BIBLIOGRAPHY

Ambrose, Stephen E. *Nothing Like It in the World: The Men Who Built the Transcontinental Railroad, 1863–1869*. New York: Simon & Schuster, 2000. Print.

Bain, David Haward. *Empire Express: Building the First Transcontinental Railroad*. New York: Viking, 1999. Print.

Central Pacific Railroad Photographic History Museum. CPRR.org, 12 Mar. 2010. Web.

Gordon, Sarah. *Passage to Union: How the Railroads Transformed American Life, 1829–1929*. Chicago: Ivan R. Dee, 1997. Print.

"Transcontinental Railroad." *American Experience*. PBS Online/ WGBH, n.d. Web.

FURTHER READINGS

Borneman, Walter R. *Rival Rails: The Race to Build America's Greatest Transcontinental Railroad*. New York: Random House, 2010. Print.

Crewe, Sabrina, and Michael V. Uschan. *The Transcontinental Railroad*. Milwaukee, WI: Gareth Stevens, 2004. Print.

Meltzer, Milton. *Hear That Train Whistle Blow! How the Railroad Changed the World*. New York: Random House, 2004. Print.

Web Links

To learn more about the transcontinental railroad, visit ABDO Publishing Company online at **www.abdopublishing.com**. Web sites about the transcontinental railroad are featured on our Book Links page. These links are routinely monitored and updated to provide the most current information available.

Places to Visit

California State Railroad Museum
125 I Street, Sacramento, CA 95814
916-445-6645
www.csrmf.org
See exhibits, documents, and restored locomotives at this California museum.

Golden Spike National Historic Site
Promontory Summit, Utah
435-471-2209 ext. 29
www.nps.gov/gosp
Visit the site where the two parts of the transcontinental railroad were ceremonially joined on May 10, 1869. Replicas of the two engines involved in the joining are on the site. Visitors can also walk on the real Big Fill and see other parts of the railroad workers' handiwork.

Union Pacific Railroad Museum
200 Pearl Street, Council Bluffs, IA 51503
712-329-8307
http://uprrmuseum.org
The museum, in the city that Abraham Lincoln named as the eastern terminus of the transcontinental railroad, houses artifacts, photographs, and documents related to the development of the railroad and the American West. Also open to the public in Council Bluffs is the 14-room mansion that Union Pacific chief engineer Grenville Dodge built for himself and his family in 1869.

Source Notes

Chapter 1. Mission Accomplished

1. Rebecca Cooper Winter. "Eastward to Promontory." *Central Pacific Railroad Photographic History Museum.* CPRR.org, n.d. Web. 6 Aug. 2010.

2. Ibid.

3. Ibid.

4. Stephen E. Ambrose. *Nothing Like It in the World: The Men Who Built the Transcontinental Railroad, 1863–1869.* New York: Simon & Schuster, 2000. Print. 362.

5. David Haward Bain. *Empire Express: Building the First Transcontinental Railroad.* New York: Viking, 1999. Print. 648.

6. "Four Special Spikes." *NPS.gov.* N.p, n.d. Web. 8 Aug. 2010.

7. David Haward Bain. *Empire Express: Building the First Transcontinental Railroad.* New York: Viking, 1999. Print. 662.

8. Ibid. 671.

Chapter 2. The Rise of the Train

1. John Debo Galloway. *The First Transcontinental Railroad: Central Pacific, Union Pacific.* New York: Simmons-Boardman, 1950. Print. 4.

2. Charles Dickens. "American Notes." *The Complete Works of Charles-Dickens.* dickens-literature.com, n.d. Web. 22 Aug. 2010.

3. Ibid.

4. Ibid.

Chapter 3. Idea Hatched; Route Chosen

1. S. W. Dexter. "Something New." *The Emigrant* 1832: 2. *Central Pacific Railroad Photographic History Museum.* Transcribed by Larry Mullaly. CPRR.org, Aug. 20, 2006. Web. 3 Nov. 2010.

2. John Debo Galloway. *The First Transcontinental Railroad: Central Pacific, Union Pacific.* New York: Simmons-Boardman, 1950. Print. 29.

3. R. A. Giusepi, ed. "Manifest Destiny." *History World International.* History World International, 2004. Web. 16 Aug. 2010.

4. Asa Whitney. *A Project for a Railroad to the Pacific.* New York: George W. Wood, 1849. 4-5. *Google Books.* Web. 10 Aug. 2010.

Chapter 4. Breaking Ground

1. Stephen E. Ambrose. *Nothing Like It in the World: The Men Who Built the Transcontinental Railroad, 1863–1869*. New York: Simon & Schuster, 2000. Print. 106.

2. "Abraham Lincoln and California." *The Lincoln Institute Presents: Abraham Lincoln's Classroom*. The Lincoln Institute, n.d. Web. 28 Aug. 2010.

3. David Haward Bain. *Empire Express: Building the First Transcontinental Railroad*. New York: Viking, 1999. Print. 163-164.

4. Stephen E. Ambrose. *Nothing Like It in the World: The Men Who Built the Transcontinental Railroad, 1863–1869*. New York: Simon & Schuster, 2000. Print. 95.

Chapter 5. Railroad Work Begins

1. Stephen E. Ambrose. *Nothing Like It in the World: The Men Who Built the Transcontinental Railroad*, 1863–1869. New York: Simon & Schuster, 2000. Print. 133.

2. "Irish Potato Famine." *The History Place*. The History Place, n.d. Web. 31 Aug. 2010.

3. Stephen E. Ambrose. *Nothing Like It in the World: The Men Who Built the Transcontinental Railroad*, 1863–1869. New York: Simon & Schuster, 2000. Print. 156.

4. Edson T. Strobridge. "The Central Pacific Railroad and the Legend of Cape Horn, 1865–1866." *Central Pacific Railroad Photographic History Museum*. CPRR.org, 2001. Web. 31 Aug. 2010.

Chapter 6. Progress Made

1. "The Race to Utah!" *American Experience*. PBS Online/WGBH, n.d. Web. 2 Sept. 2010.

2. Ibid.

3. John R. Gilliss. "Tunnels of the Pacific Railroad." *Van Nostrand's Eclectic Engineering Magazine* II (1870). *Central Pacific Railroad Photographic History Museum*. CPRR.org, n.d. Web. 31 Aug. 2010.

4. Ibid.

5. "Central Pacific Railroad Timeline." *Sierra Nevada Virtual Museum*. N.p, n.d. Web. 2 Sept. 2010.

6. "The Race to Utah!" *American Experience*. PBS Online/WGBH, n.d. Web. 2 Sept. 2010.

SOURCE NOTES CONTINUED

7. J. K. Medbery. "Our Pacific Railroads." *The Atlantic Monthly* 20:122 (December 1867). *Making of America.* Cornell University Library, n.d. Web. 16 Oct. 2010.

8. Stephen E. Ambrose. *Nothing Like It in the World: The Men Who Built the Transcontinental Railroad, 1863–1869.* New York: Simon & Schuster, 2000. Print. 346.

Chapter 7. Land Battles and Continuing the Work

1. "The Race to Utah!" *American Experience.* PBS Online/WGBH, n.d. Web. 2 Sept. 2010.

2. "William Tecumseh Sherman." *New Perspectives on the West.* The West Film Project and WETA, n.d. Web. 6 Sept. 2010.

3. Ibid.

4. "Central Pacific Railroad Timeline." *Sierra Nevada Virtual Museum.* N.p, n.d. Web. 2 Sept. 2010.

5. "Building the Union Pacific." *Wyoming Tales and Trails.* G. B. Dobson, n.d. Web. 6 Sept. 2010.

Chapter 8. The Final Stretch

1. Stephen E. Ambrose. *Nothing Like It in the World: The Men Who Built the Transcontinental Railroad, 1863–1869.* New York: Simon & Schuster, 2000. Print. 322.

2. Ibid.

3. "Promontory." *KUED.* 2002. N.p., n.d. Web. 6 Sept. 2010.

4. David Haward Bain. *Empire Express: Building the First Transcontinental Railroad.* New York: Viking, 1999. Print. 639.

5. Ibid.

6. Stephen E. Ambrose. *Nothing Like It in the World: The Men Who Built the Transcontinental Railroad, 1863–1869.* New York: Simon & Schuster, 2000. Print. 355.

Chapter 9. The Effects of the Railroad

1. Stephen E. Ambrose. *Nothing Like It in the World: The Men Who Built the Transcontinental Railroad, 1863–1869.* New York: Simon & Schuster, 2000. Print. 370.

2. "Transcontinental Railroad." *Exploring the West.* Stanford University, n.d. Web. 11 Sept. 2010.

INDEX

Index Continued

About the Author

Diane Marczely Gimpel is a freelance writer and former daily newspaper reporter. She lives outside Philadelphia, Pennsylvania, with her family.

Photo Credits

AP Images, cover, 3, 11, 42, 96; Andrew Russell/AP Images, 6; Hulton Archive/Stringer/Getty Images, 13, 24, 95; Science & Society Picture Library/Contributor/Getty Images, 14, 23; MPI/Stringer/Getty Images, 18, 31, 51, 71, 77, 97 (top); Rich Pedroncelli/AP Images, 32; A. J. Russell/AP Images, 37; Anthony Berger/Library of Congress, 41, 97 (bottom); Andrew J. Russell/Library of Congress, 46, 52, 74, 98; Alfred A. Hart/Library of Congress, 56, 73, 99 (top); North Wind Picture Archives, 63; Theodore R. Davis/Library of Congress, 64; A. J. Russell/Stringer/Getty Images, 80; Fotosearch/Stringer/Getty Images, 83, 99 (bottom); Tim Schoon/AP Images, 84; John Badman/AP Images, 91